in the
sixties

in the
sixties

Frank Habicht

AXIS PUBLISHING

First published in Great Britain in 1998 by
AXIS PUBLISHING
8 The Arena, Mollison Avenue
Enfield, Middlesex, EN3 7NJ, UK

First published in New Zealand in 1998 by
TANDEM PRESS
2 Rugby Road, Birkenhead, North Shore City,
New Zealand

Copyright © Frank Habicht

ISBN 1 870845 30 7

Cover design: Christine Hansen
Book design: Christine Hansen
Cover production: Archer Design
Electronic Reproduction: Image Centre Auckland, New Zealand
Printed and bound: Everbest, Hong Kong

foreword

I am by nature a nostalgic person who values the past. As novelist L.P. Hartley wrote in the riveting first sentence of his most famous novel *The Go Between,* 'The past is a foreign country, they do things differently there.' Looking at Frank's evocative photographs I am transported back to a London that, in less than three decades, has ceased to exist. (What bliss to see no parking meters or those modern iron maidens for motorists, the clamp!) There is even a photograph of myself and my wife, admittedly taken in Ireland which, with my over-long sixties haircut and safari jacket, puts me irrevocably in a time warp – a faded replica that Madame Tussaud's forgot to melt down! Thanks, Frank, for reminding me never to dress like that again.

Frank has a sure poet's eye for the 'moment of truth' that all good photographers seek and few achieve, his technique concealing the technique. Young and old are captured by his lens in those fleeting milliseconds of unawareness that make for great shots. Those of us who lived through the so-called Swinging Sixties need to be reminded that it was the first time after the end of the war that we felt the chains of austerity fall away. It is perhaps forgotten that food rationing continued for many years after the cessation of hostilities, that although Atlee's Labour government ushered in a social revolution, it was tempered by the fact that Britain was emotionally and financially bankrupt. People were tired, all the major cities still bore the scars of the Blitz, there was a housing shortage, clothes were drab – we had won the war, but peace had not delivered the promised land.

Then, crawling towards a mirage that proved to be real, we found ourselves again. The Carnaby Street era appeared to happen overnight as a generation took to the streets and said, 'Enough is enough, we're only young once and we intend to enjoy it.' What was it, this feeling that overtook us? Was it the Beatles who shook their perfect, uniform hairdos at convention and changed the face of pop music? Was it the Flower People,

v

the CND marchers, or Mary Quant who altered the shape of all those delectable dolly birds? Or was it a combination of all these factors coming together at the same time by a chance of history? Whatever the true answer we were never to be the same again. We started to believe that the long years of war and deprivation had not been in vain, we had an identity at last. Prefabricated houses were replaced by bricks and mortar, new cars that didn't look like prehistoric monsters started to appear, the bomb sites were cleared at last, and the BBC gave us *That Was The Week That Was*.

It was Frank's destiny to be around to point his camera at this time, and to give succeeding generations a glimpse of a society in transition. Most artists have no conscious awareness that they are recording for posterity – usually they are more concerned with earning a crust, and it is only afterwards that their work takes on an added significance. For me, though, Frank's portfolio does have significance, for it captures the exuberance and innocence of those gilded years, and if he did not achieve the universal fame of a Bailey or Donovan, or gain the covers of *Vogue*, he never lowered his standards or settled for the second rate. It is his feel for *place* as well as his subjects that gives this book a unique freshness and evokes the spirit of those lost times.

He and I bridge the years. Each of us in our separate ways was part of those halcyon days, and I consider it a privilege to have been asked to introduce his work to a new audience. The camera can and does lie on many occasions, but I can attest to the fact that these photographs are the real thing. This is how it was. This is how it will never be again. We are older, but we remember the time when brightness fell from the air.

— **Bryan Forbes**

pictures for Anna

'Once upon a time in the sixties…'

Words don't come easy, time fades, some images clearly anchored in the mind, time as partner and opponent, relics of an overwhelming colourful and beautiful time…. The Sixties reflecting on yesterday's tales and realities. Some imprints edited and framed were taken out of sheer devotion and tender concern for the subject matter. A retrospective view of an exhilarating period, a view of our perceptions and dreams, a diversity of individuals, the uniformity of classes, relationships, the faces of famous and common people, the charm of childhood and models with no inhibitions. It seemingly was an époque granting eternal youth. A passion for life not driven by commercial success, not being aware of the formal camera techniques and the lens as an extension of the eye being curious and interested in what happened here and there. The process of observation always continued…. It was simply a love affair with people and images.

'Yesterday is far away….' The Roaring Twenties were Vienna, Berlin and New Orleans. The Permissive Sixties highlighted London, Paris and New York. The Sixties heralded a new world of material affluence after the thrift and reconstruction of the Fifties. We were emerging from the ashes of the war.

London became the first swinging capital of the world with a new aristocracy of filmmakers, pop singers, models and photographers whose credentials were that they were talented, classless and young. The conventional art circles were rocked, the older order disregarded. Fresh standards were set and expressed in their own terms: 'Let every human being do his own thing'. 'We love you' sang the Rolling Stones, who projected England's new image. A highly individualised process of self-investigation, self-discovery and self-realisation was characteristic. We were lured with temptation, and not ruled by regulations and restrictions. We were all strong, young and lively, in love with life, hard-working, having fun, wanting everything that man, woman and child ever wanted. Love, security, prospects…. Above all, we

valued our newly won freedom. We could do without the awful bittersweet excitement of war. We linked arms with Vanessa Redgrave and carried our protest against the Vietnam War. We had insight, courage, and we experimented.... The only absolute commandment was the commandment of love — living in tolerance of each other, no matter what creed or colour of skin. Morality had become a matter for individual conscience. The atmosphere of frankness, sexual freedom and flower power were barometer high at the time. Exotic corners of the world were rediscovered — Puna, the 'In' place for meditation. It simply was a 'Magical Mystery Tour' while founding new capitals of freedom. We danced into the dawn... enjoying 'A Hard Day's Night'.

We linked hearts with Sandie Shaw, indestructible, a sad barefoot singer, daughter of a welder, who won a silver disc with her first hit 'There's Always Something There to Remind Me' which reached number one and sold over a quarter of a million copies; her songs were seeping from transistors all over Europe.

Vanessa Redgrave left gaudy impressions of life in Antonioni's psychedelic mystery story *Blow Up,* and starred as Isadora Duncan in Karl Reiz's epic film.

We were admiring of Franco Nero, an actor with a face of significance and a curious driving appeal. He has been named as one of the most popular actors in the Sixties.

Horror movies became a new business. The master of shock was Dracula impersonator Christopher Lee. Narcissistic and self indulgent... a magician of illusions. People like to be frightened.

Marty Feldman was of bizarre appearance, a top comedian with a tremendous sense of humour. A performer with noticeable qualities, distressed when halted in his tornado — remembered as kind and sensitive.

At any given moment Roman Polanski was plotting a film with artistic and creative abilities yet little regard for authenticity. It's the unexplored territory waiting for his mind and camera which makes him start the next film.

Writer and film director Bryan Forbes created thought-provoking movies like *The L-Shaped Room* and *Raging Moon.* His films are exciting for the eye, having grace, balance, tension and visual wit. The decade projected poetry and craziness that is still uncorrupted, honest and pure. The steep road to fame, rewarding and also paved with emotional darkness. The beat goes on, the philosophy remains. Rock protests everything and seals its wistful spirituality with affirmation.

A new age of technology dawns on us, we live with the truth of today, still in search for direction. The Sixties almost unchallenged through three decades. The Maharashi once said, 'Enjoy what you are, the natural state of man is joy'.

We were in historical terms 'les enfants terribles'. We look at ourselves as 'les enfants du paradis'.

Accept these pictures of past dreams in reply to your caring thoughts.

Time, temps — tant et tant...

Always yours

Frank Habicht

16

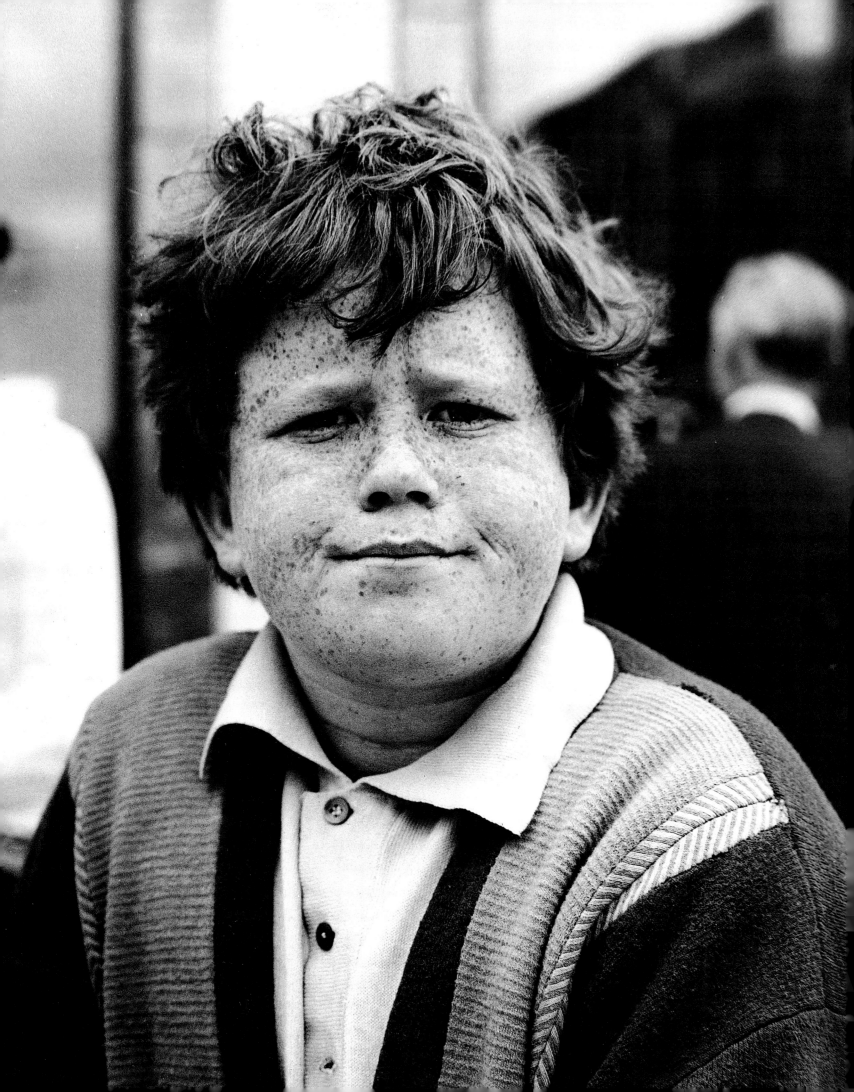

The permissive sixties . . .

49

Captions

11
Goodbye Sunshine. London 1967

12
What is in — what is out. Chelsea 1966

13
Hey Mister... City of London 1966

14
Keeping up appearances. Kings Road 1967

15
Come and join us. Salvation Army. Chelsea 1967

16
Leaving tomorrow behind. Mata Hari Boutique, Earls Court 1967

17
Reconnaissance. Bazaar Boutique, Kings Road 1967

18
Togetherness. London Eastend 1966

19
A place to be. Carol, derelict Danish Embassy, Whitechapel 1966

20
Les enfants terribles. London Eastend 1966

21
Isn't life strange... Young stall holder, Portobello Market

22
Where time stood still. Off Portobello Road 1965

23
Seeking wisdom, Portobello Market 1965

24
The heart swells with joy. Jane London, actress, Belgravia 1967

25
Flower power. Hyde Park 1969

27
Once upon a time... Hyde Park 1967

28
Live it to the hilt. René, Westminster Bridge 1968

29
Royal Guards. Horse Guard parade 1968

30/31
Ocean full of faces. Janet Stevens, actress, Paddington 1967

32
Saturday night... Swiss Gate 1968

33
Sunday morning... Earls Court 1968

34
Beyond the yellow brick road. Ingrid Boulting, actress. Victoria Embankment 1968

35
Jeanette Lang, model, Fulham Road 1968

36
We are... street buskers... Portobello Road 1967

37
Art student. Central School of Art, High Holborn 1966

38/39
Life at the top. Photographer's open-air studio, Courtfield Gardens

40/41
Made for each other. Paul and Joan, Courtfield Gardens 1967

42
Anti-Vietnam war demonstration. Vanessa Redgrave, film actress

43
Tarique Ali, student protest leader. Trafalgar Square 1968

44
Anti-Vietnam war demonstration. Grosvenor Square 1968

45
Peace message. Vanessa Redgrave, Grosvenor Square 1968

46
La rouge et la noire. Grosvenor Square 1968

47
Fair cop. Grosvenor Square 1968

48
Queens Birthday Parade 1968

49
And who won... Horse Guard parade 1968

50
Freedom of speech. Hyde Park 1967

51
I'm the Gypsy — the Acid Queen. Derelict churchyard near St. Pauls' 1968

52
Satisfaction. Rolling Stones concert, Hyde Park 1969

53
And the crowd went crazy... Rolling Stones concert, Hyde Park 1969

54
I am a sensation. Keith Richards/Rolling Stones 1969

55
Incomparable. Rolling Stones 1969

56/57
Part of the scene... Rolling Stones concert 1969

58/59
I like it. Yes I do. Open-air festival, Wroteham Park Estate 1967

60/61
Silence is Golden.Pop group 1968

63
Bare encounter. Near Knightsbridge 1969

64/65
Facing life bravely. Courtfield Gardens 1967

66
Bed-sitter girl. Earls Court 1967

67
Do you think it's alright... Earls Court 1967

68
Till death us do part. Photographer's rooftop 1969

69
My gentle lady. Off Kings Road 1968

70
The morning after. Liz Romanoff, film actress, Knightsbridge Mews 1969

71
Accepting one's fate. London Eastend 1969

72
Linda and Paula. Top Models Agency 1969

73
Sensuous nude 1969

74
Reassurance. Tina, Courtfield Gardens studio 1969

75
Joan Ferguson, fashion designer, Courtfield Gardens studio 1969

76/77
Marriage a la mode. Advertising assignment 1968

78
Mystic — self images. Derelict churchyard, Tower Bridge

79
Aylesbury Estate 1967

80
Where the minds meet. Pimlico district 1969

81
Rachel. Cork, Ireland 1969

82
Where the minds can't usually go. Derelict church, Tower Bridge 1967

83
It's a wonderful place. Photographer and German model Uschi, Epping Forest 1966

84
Private art collections. Connie Kreski, '69 Playmate of the Year, Mayfair 1969

85
Hylette Adolph, top model, Kensington 1969

86
Femme totale. Kate O'Mara, film actress, South London 1969

87
Les mademoiselles. Children of actor Claude Riche 1968

88
Bare essentials. George and models, Courtfield Gardens 1968

89
Permissive paradise. Harrington Gardens 1967

90
Sweets for my Sweet... Connie Kreski, Mayfair 1969

91
Delicacy. Connie Kreski, Mayfair 1969

92
Double, double, toil and trouble. Roman Polanski, film director, *Macbeth* film set 1969

93
Macbeth film set, Pinewood Studios 1969

94/95
Linda Hayden and Yvonne Paul, actresses, *Devils Touch*. Medieval film production 1968

96
Living the moment. Bryan Forbes, writer and film director, and Nanette Newman, actress Cork Film Festival 1969

97
Rachel Williams, model. Cork Film Festival 1969

98/99
Franco Nero, film actor, *Virgin and the Gypsy*. Film set 1967

100/101
Sammy Davis Jr. and friend. Kings Road 1968

102/103
Christopher Lee, Dracula performer, and family. Belgravia

104
Voulez vous un rendezvous. Alexandra Bastedo, actress1969

105
Lady in white. Alexandra Bastedo, actress

106
Scepticism. Child study 1967

107
Marty Feldman, film actor and comedian 1969

108
Each moment forever, Janette Stevens and worker 1968

109
Lesley Anne Down, film actress 1968

111
Mesmerized by just the sight. Connie Kreski, Mayfair 1969

112
Total absorption. Uncredited 1969

113
Lord Lichfield, photographer, Kensington Close 1968

114/115
Puppet on a String. Sandie Shaw, pop singer, Pimlico 1968

116
And live happily ever after. Rehearsing, Wimbledon Park 1967